COUNTRY PROFILES

CHINA

BY EMILY ROSE OACHS

BELLWETHER MEDIA • MINNEAPOLIS, MN

Blastoff! Discovery launches
a new mission: reading to learn.
Filled with facts and features, each
book offers you an exciting new
world to explore!

This edition first published in 2018 by Bellwether Media, Inc.

No part of this publication may be reproduced in whole or in part
without written permission of the publisher.
For information regarding permission, write to Bellwether Media, Inc.,
Attention: Permissions Department,
5357 Penn Avenue South, Minneapolis, MN 55419.

Library of Congress Cataloging-in-Publication Data

Names: Oachs, Emily Rose, author.
Title: China / by Emily Rose Oachs.
Description: Minneapolis, MN : Bellwether Media, Inc., 2018.
 | Series: Blastoff! Discovery: Country Profiles | Includes
   bibliographical references and index. | Audience: Grades 3-8. |
   Audience: Ages 7-13.
Identifiers: LCCN 2016053598 (print) | LCCN 2016055671
   (ebook) | ISBN 9781626176782 (hardcover : alkaline paper) |
   ISBN 9781681034089 (ebook)
Subjects: LCSH: China–Juvenile literature.
Classification: LCC DS706 .O25 2018 (print) | LCC DS706 (ebook)
   | DDC 951–dc23
LC record available at https://lccn.loc.gov/2016053598

Editor: Christina Leaf   Designer: Brittany McIntosh

Printed in the United States of America, North Mankato, MN.

TABLE OF CONTENTS

THE GREAT WALL OF CHINA

A large group of people stands in the shadow of the Great Wall of China. The broad, sturdy wall towers high overhead. For many **dynasties**, the wall kept out enemies. Today, it hosts millions of sightseers each year.

OTHER TOP SITES

FORBIDDEN CITY

MOUNT EVEREST

ORIENTAL PEARL TOWER

TERRA-COTTA ARMY

The group climbs the wall's ancient steps. From the top, the visitors admire the wall snaking along the hilltops of China's countryside. Commanding watchtowers stand along its length. In the distance, they see where the wall disappears into the horizon. Welcome to China!

China stretches from central Asia to the continent's eastern edge. It is the fourth-largest country in the world, spreading across 3,705,407 square miles (9,596,960 square kilometers). Fourteen countries touch China. These include Russia and Mongolia to the north and India to the southwest. The waters of the Yellow, East China, and South China Seas wash onto China's eastern shores.

Beijing, the nation's capital, is located in northeastern China. The cities of Macau and Hong Kong spread onto islands off China's southern coast. Close by stands Hainan Island. The Chinese island of Taiwan sits to China's southeast.

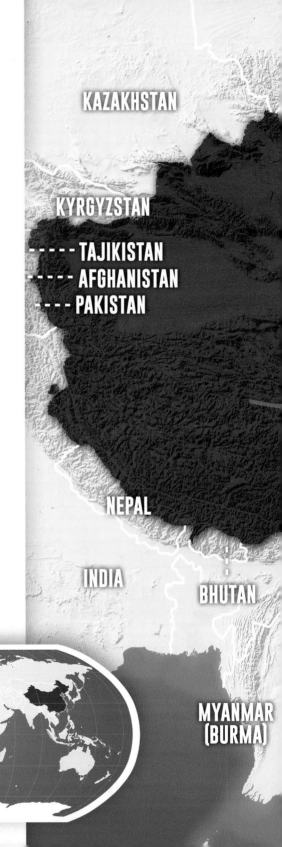

KAZAKHSTAN

KYRGYZSTAN

TAJIKISTAN
AFGHANISTAN
PAKISTAN

NEPAL

INDIA

BHUTAN

MYANMAR
(BURMA)

TIME ZONES

China is more than 3,000 miles (4,828 kilometers) wide. Yet the entire country is within the same time zone. This means that in some areas, the sun may set at midnight!

RUSSIA
MONGOLIA
BEIJING
NORTH KOREA
CHINA
HUANG HE RIVER
YELLOW SEA
SHANGHAI
CHONGQING
YANGTZE RIVER
EAST CHINA SEA
HONG KONG
TAIWAN
GUANGZHOU
MACAU
N
W
E
S
VIETNAM
LAOS
SOUTH CHINA SEA
HAINAN

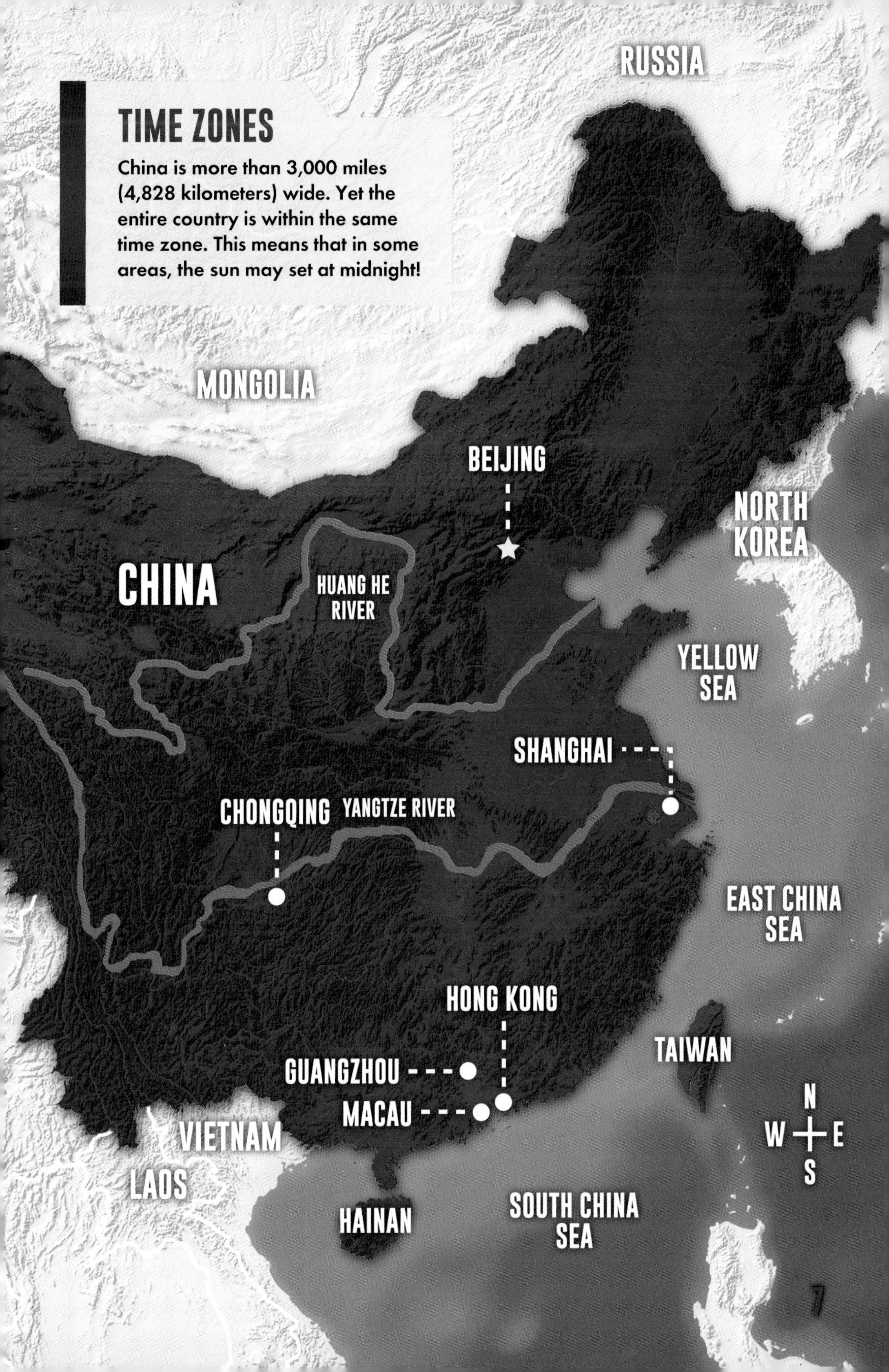

LANDSCAPE AND CLIMATE

Northwestern China is mostly flat and dry. The broad Gobi Desert sits in the north. In the far west rests the Taklimakan Desert. Mountains crisscross much of China's land. The cold, towering Himalayas trail along China's southwestern border. Among them, the world's highest peak, Mount Everest, stands between China and Nepal.

MT. EVEREST

= TIBETAN PLATEAU
= DESERT   = HIMALAYAS

N
W + E
S

GOBI DESERT

TIBETAN PLATEAU

ROOF OF THE WORLD

In some areas, the Tibetan Plateau stands around 16,500 feet (5,029 meters) above sea level. This lofty height earned it the nickname "the roof of the world."

YANGTZE RIVER

BEIJING
Average
seasonal highs
and lows

JANUARY
HIGH: 32 °F (0 °C)
LOW: 19 °F (-7 °C)

APRIL
HIGH: 68 °F (20 °C)
LOW: 45 °F (7 °C)

JULY
HIGH: 88 °F (31 °C)
LOW: 72 °F (22 °C)

OCTOBER
HIGH: 68 °F (20 °C)
LOW: 46 °F (8 °C)

°F = degrees Fahrenheit
°C = degrees Celsius

    The Tibetan **Plateau** covers southwestern China.
There, the lengthy Yangtze and Huang He rivers form.
They flow across the low, rolling **plains** of China's
eastern **provinces**. In late spring, **monsoons** bring
rain to eastern China. The dry season comes each winter.

China's varied landscape holds many different animals. In central China, giant pandas munch on bamboo in mountain forests. Golden monkeys and goat-like takins also roam these areas. In the **rugged** Himalayas, rare snow leopards hunt blue sheep. Ibex wander western mountains.

The Yangtze River is home to **endangered** Chinese alligators, giant salamanders, and paddlefish. In the **tropical** southeast, the Chinese pangolin searches for termite nests in forests and grasslands. **Venomous** king cobras slither through the trees of southern China's **rain forests**.

TAKIN

CHINESE PANGOLIN

KING COBRA

GOLDEN MONKEY

KING COBRAS

King cobras release powerful venom when they bite. Just one bite from a king cobra could kill an elephant!

GIANT
PANDA - - - -

GIANT PANDA

Life Span: 20 years
Red List Status: vulnerable

giant panda range = ■

LEAST CONCERN	NEAR THREATENED	VULNERABLE	ENDANGERED	CRITICALLY ENDANGERED	EXTINCT IN THE WILD	EXTINCT

POPULATION

No other country in the world has a population as large as China. About one out of every five people in the world live there!

More than 1.3 billion people call China home. The country's population is made up of 56 different groups of people. About nine out of every ten Chinese people are Han, the largest group. Other smaller groups include the Zhuang, Mongols, and Tibetans.

Each **ethnic** group has its own **traditions** and language. Most Chinese people also speak Mandarin, the official language. China is an **atheist** country. Still, many people practice Buddhism or folk religions.

FAMOUS FACE

Name: Yao Ming
Birthday: September 12, 1980
Hometown: Shanghai, China
Famous for: All-star player for the Houston Rockets of the National Basketball Association (NBA) from 2002 to 2011, and a member of the Naismith Memorial Basketball Hall of Fame

SPEAK MANDARIN

Mandarin uses characters instead of letters. However, Mandarin words can be written with the English alphabet so you can read them.

ENGLISH	MANDARIN	HOW TO SAY IT
hello	ni hao	nee HAOW
goodbye	zai jian	tsai JYEN
please	qing	ching
thank you	xie xie	SHYEH-shyeh
yes	shi	shih
no	bu	booh

COMMUNITIES

Family is extremely important to the Chinese. Most families are small, with no more than two children. Grandparents often live with their children and may help care for their grandchildren.

BEIJING

RURAL CHINA

Small apartments are common in the large, crowded cities. Wealthy people may buy larger apartments in high-rise buildings. Bicycles or motorcycles help city dwellers get from place to place. Cars, subways, and buses are also popular. In countryside villages, the Chinese often live in homes of wood, stone, or bricks made of mud. Highways and railroads connect the country. **Rural** Chinese people may also use cart paths or waterways to get around.

To greet others, the Chinese may offer a gentle handshake or nod their heads. They often seem reserved. Modesty is highly valued in Chinese society. Often, the Chinese try to **downplay** their achievements. When receiving praise, a person may brush it aside. It is not considered polite to boast about successes.

Many Chinese people wear Western-style clothes. But on special occasions, they may dress in traditional clothing. Women wear dresses called *cheongsams*, while men put on pants and long *changshan* robes.

CHEONGSAMS

The Chinese value education greatly. All children must attend school for at least nine years. At age 6, Chinese children enter primary school. After five or six years, students move on to secondary school. Some students complete more than the required secondary school. Graduates must pass a difficult test to go on to university.

Many Chinese adults work on farms. Rice, wheat, and tea are common crops. China also has a large manufacturing industry. Factory workers produce steel, aircraft, and cars. Electronics and clothing are major **exports**. Along the coasts, fishing is a key industry. **Service jobs** are also common in China.

CAR FACTORY

RICE FARMING

PRACTICING THE
MARTIAL ART *QI GONG*

Martial arts, such as *kung fu* and *wushu*, are popular in China. Each morning, millions of young and old alike fill China's parks to practice *tai chi*. In this martial art, people slowly flow through a pattern of movements. Other widespread sports include badminton, soccer, and basketball.

PING-PONG SUPERSTARS

China is famous for its excellence in table tennis, or ping-pong. Since 1988, Chinese athletes have won 28 of the 32 Olympic gold medals in the sport!

Many Chinese people enjoy singing **karaoke** with friends. They also pass the time watching television or playing video games. Often, friends meet up to play *mah-jongg* or the chess-like game of *xiangqi*.

MAH-JONGG

CHINESE LANTERN ACTIVITY

What You Need:
- colored construction paper
- scissors
- stapler
- glue (optional)
- glitter, wrapping paper, other decorations (optional)

Instructions:
1. Cut off and save a 1-inch (2.5-centimeter) strip from the short end of the piece of paper.
2. Fold the paper in half the long way.
3. From the folded side, cut toward the opposite edge. Make nine cuts about 1 inch (2.5 centimeters) apart. They should stop about 1 inch (2.5 centimeters) from the edge.
4. Optional: Decorate the top and bottom borders
5. Unfold the paper, and roll it into a fat tube so the edges overlap. Staple the edges to hold the lantern's shape.
6. Staple the strip of paper saved from step 1 onto the lantern

GUANGDONG BREAKFASTS

In Guangdong, a breakfast tradition is *dim sum*. Family and friends socialize over many small dishes, such as buns or shrimp dumplings. They sip tea as they eat and chat!

Tea is served with almost every meal in China. Rice and noodles are also important **staples** in Chinese diets. A special dish is Peking duck. This meal features thin slices of roasted duck with a sweet sauce and thin pancakes.

For breakfast, steamed buns and a rice porridge called *congee* are common. People dine on simple meals for lunch. A typical dinner includes soup, rice or noodles, and dishes of vegetables and meat. The Chinese use chopsticks instead of forks to pick up food.

CONGEE

PEKING DUCK

JIAOZI RECIPE

Ingredients:
about 50 round dumpling wrappers
1-2 pounds uncooked ground pork
1 tablespoon ginger root, minced
2 tablespoons green onion, sliced
1 tablespoon sesame oil
5 cups Chinese cabbage, finely shredded
salt and pepper
water

Steps:
1. Mix the ground meat, green onion, ginger, sesame oil, and a pinch of salt and pepper into a large bowl. Add the cabbage, and stir it all together.

2. Hold a dumpling wrapper in your hand. Fill it with 1 to 2 teaspoons of the filling. Use water to dampen the edges of the wrapper. Then, fold the wrapper in half. Pinch the edges closed. Set it aside.

3. Repeat until there is no filling left.

4. With an adult, boil water. Place the dumplings into the water, and stir every so often. Let them cook for several minutes. Floating dumplings means they are ready to eat! Enjoy them with soy sauce or rice vinegar.

CELEBRATIONS

Chinese New Year is China's most important holiday. The 15 days of celebration begin in late January or February. They bring family dinners, parades, and fireworks. Young people receive red envelopes filled with money. On the final day, the Chinese light colorful lanterns and watch lion dances for the Lantern Festival.

During April's *Qing Ming* Festival, people clean the graves of family members. They then leave offerings of food and yellow paper representing money. The Dragon Boat Festival usually comes in June. People race dragon-shaped rowboats during this ancient festival. On October 1, National Day honors China's formation. Military parades and fireworks show the pride the Chinese have for their nation!

DRAGON BOAT FESTIVAL

CELEBRATING THE MOON

Each fall, the Mid-Autumn Festival draws people together to worship the full moon. Families gather for feasts and to appreciate the bright, round moon while eating mooncakes!

CHINESE NEW YEAR LANTERN FESTIVAL

有凤采

A phoenix comes with

1211 CE
China invaded by Mongol armies

2070 BCE
Xia dynasty, China's first dynasty, is established

221 BCE
All of China is unified for the first time under the Qin dynasty

1600s
End of more than 2,000 years of construction on the Great Wall

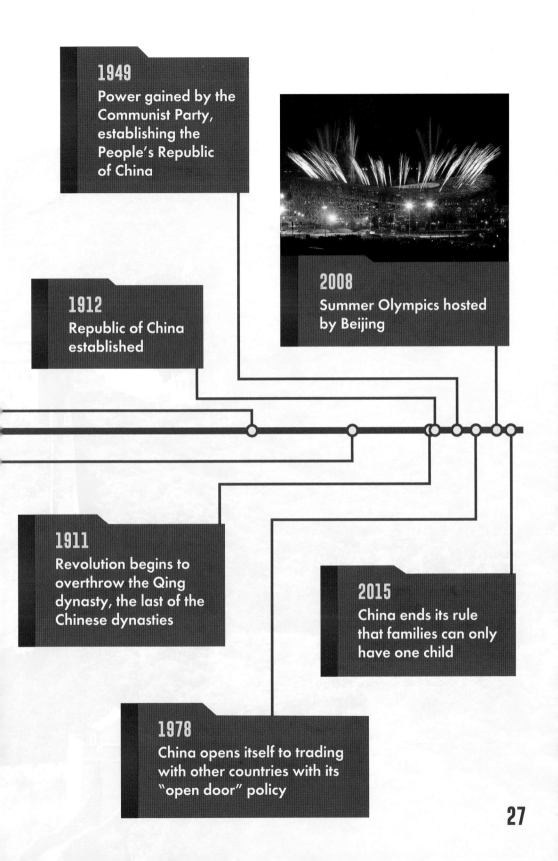

1949
Power gained by the Communist Party, establishing the People's Republic of China

2008
Summer Olympics hosted by Beijing

1912
Republic of China established

1911
Revolution begins to overthrow the Qing dynasty, the last of the Chinese dynasties

2015
China ends its rule that families can only have one child

1978
China opens itself to trading with other countries with its "open door" policy

CHINA FACTS

Official Name: People's Republic of China

Flag of China: China's flag has a red background. A large yellow star stands in the upper left corner. Four smaller yellow stars curve around its right side. Red stands for revolution. The large star is a symbol for the Communist Party. The smaller stars represent the four social classes of China. China adopted this flag in 1949.

Area: 3,705,407 square miles
(9,596,960 square kilometers)

Capital City: Beijing

Important Cities: Shanghai, Chongqing, Guangzhou, Tianjin, Shenzhen

Population:
1,373,541,278 (July 2016)

WHERE PEOPLE LIVE

COUNTRYSIDE
44.4%

CITY
55.6%

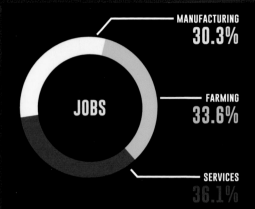

MANUFACTURING
30.3%

JOBS

FARMING
33.6%

SERVICES
36.1%

Main Exports:

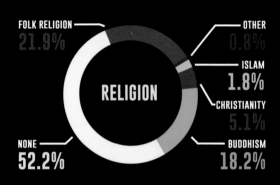

clothing   food   fabric

toys   electronics   furniture

National Holiday:
National Day (October 1)

Main Language:
Mandarin

Form of Government:
communism

Title for Country Leader:
president

FOLK RELIGION
21.9%

OTHER
0.8%

ISLAM
1.8%

RELIGION

CHRISTIANITY
5.1%

NONE
52.2%

BUDDHISM
18.2%

Unit of Money:
Yuan; ten *jiao* make up one yuan.

GLOSSARY

atheist—believing that God does not exist

downplay—to make something sound less important than it is

dynasties—lines of rulers that come from the same family

endangered—at risk of becoming extinct

ethnic—related to a group of people who share customs and an identity

exports—products sold by one country to another

karaoke—an activity in which people sing along to popular songs

martial arts—styles and techniques of fighting and self-defense that are practiced as sport

monsoons—winds that shift direction each season; monsoons bring heavy rain.

plains—large areas of flat land

plateau—an area of flat, raised land

provinces—areas within a country; provinces follow all the laws of the country and make some of their own laws.

rain forests—thick, green forests that receive a lot of rain

rugged—rough and uneven

rural—related to the countryside

service jobs—jobs that perform tasks for people or businesses

staples—widely used foods or other items

traditions—customs, ideas, or beliefs handed down from one generation to the next

tropical—part of the tropics; the tropics is a hot, rainy region near the equator.

venomous—producing a poisonous substance called venom

TO LEARN MORE

AT THE LIBRARY

Capek, Michael. *Secrets of the Terracotta Army: Tomb of an Ancient Chinese Emperor.* North Mankato, Minn.: Capstone Press, 2015.

Demuth, Patricia Brennan. *Where Is the Great Wall?* New York, N.Y.: Grosset & Dunlap, 2015.

Liu, Na, and Andrés Vera Martínez. *Little White Duck: A Childhood in China.* Minneapolis, Minn.: Graphic Universe, 2012.

ON THE WEB

Learning more about China is as easy as 1, 2, 3.

1. Go to www.factsurfer.com.

2. Enter "China" into the search box.

3. Click the "Surf" button and you will see a list of related web sites.

With factsurfer.com, finding more information is just a click away.

INDEX

The images in this book are reproduced through the courtesy of: Alan Bauman, front cover, pp. 5 (middle bottom), 8 (inset), 10 (top), 13 (bottom), 23 (top upper), 29 (currency); Juan Martinez, front cover (flag), pp. 8, 19 (top), 23 (bottom), 28 (flag), 29 (coin); eXpose, pp. 4-5; Peter Zaharov, p. 5 (top middle); Neale Cousland, p. 5 (bottom); Tony V, p. 5 (top); Brittany McIntosh, pp. 6-7; shuige/ Getty Images, p. 9 (inset); ESB Professional, pp. 9 (inset), 14; Little Carol, p. 10 (middle); Trong Nguyen, pp. 10-11; Zeng Wei Jun, p. 10 (bottom corner); Alina MD, p. 10 (bottom); Dmitry Kalinovsky, p. 12; ZUMA Press, Inc./ Alamy Stock Photo, p. 13 (top); Tipwam, p. 15; Visual Space, p. 16; Xinhua/ Alamy Stock Photo, p. 17; Junrong, p. 18; Hung Chung Chih, pp. 19 (bottom), 26; VCG/ Contributor/ Getty Images, p. 20 (bottom); Oleksiy Maksymenko/ GLOW Images, p. 20 (top); Axel Bueckert, p. 21 (top); Hemis/ Alamy Stock Photo, p. 22; Kheng Guan Toh, p. 23 (top lower); Windmoon, p. 24; Saravut Khusrisuwan, p. 25 (inset); Zhao Jian Kang, p. 25; Everett Collection Inc/ Alamy Stock Photo, p. 27.